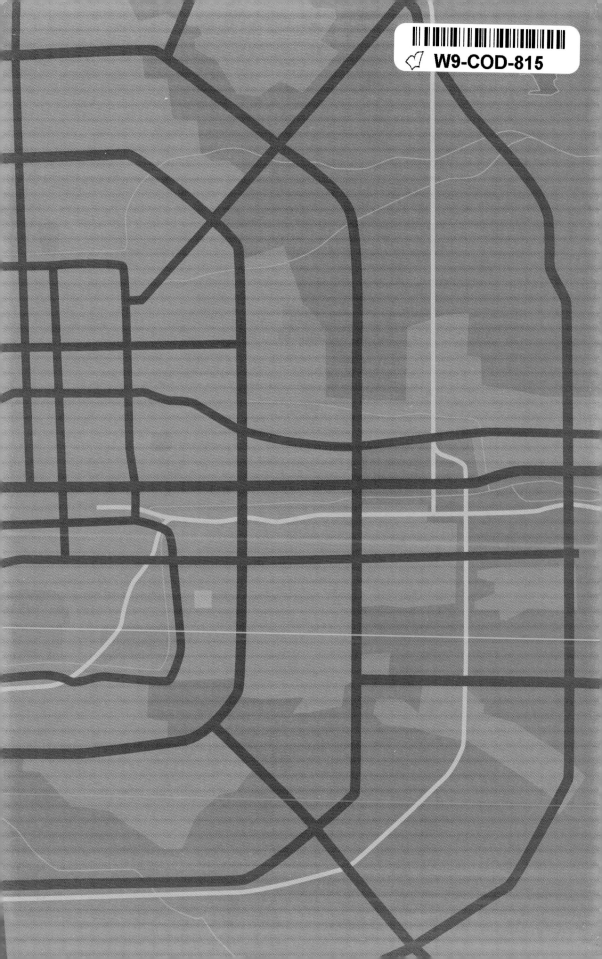
W9-COD-815

Global Cities
BEIJING

Nancy Pellegrini
photographs by Adrian Cooper

CHELSEA HOUSE
PUBLISHERS
An imprint of Infobase Publishing

Beijing

Copyright 2007 © by Evans Brothers Limited

Chelsea House
An imprint of Infobase Publishing
132 West 31st Street
New York NY 10001

            Library of Congress Cataloging-in-Publication Data
Pellegrini, Nancy.
  Beijing / Nancy Pellegrini ; photographs by Adrian Cooper.
      p. cm. — (Global cities)
  Includes bibliographical references and index.
  ISBN 0-7910-8848-0 (alk. paper)
  1. Beijing (China)—Juvenile literature. I. Cooper, Adrian. II. Title.
III. Series.

  DS795.P385 2007
  951'.156—dc22   2006029501

Designer: Simon Walster, Big Blu Design
Maps and graphics: Martin Darlinson

All photographs are by Adrian Cooper (EASI-Images).

First published by Evans Brothers Limited
2A Portman Mansions, Chiltern Street, London W1U 6NR, United
Kingdom

This edition published under license from Evans Brothers Limited.
All rights reserved.

Contents

Living in an urban world

Some time in 2007, history will be made. For the first time ever, the world's population becomes more urban than rural. An estimated 3.3 billion people are now living in towns and cities, and for many, it's a fairly new experience. In China, for example, the number of people living in urban areas increased from 196 million in 1980 to over 536 million in 2005.

The urban challenge...

The shift to a mainly urban population is being repeated around the world and provides a complex set of challenges for the 21st century. Many challenges are local: providing clean water for the people of expanding cities, for example. Other challenges are global. The spread of diseases in tightly packed cities is a problem, as it is between cities linked by air routes, high-speed trains, and roads. Pollution from urban areas is another concern, because urban residents tend to generate more pollution than their rural counterparts.

▼ The position of Beijing in relation to China and, inset, other countries.

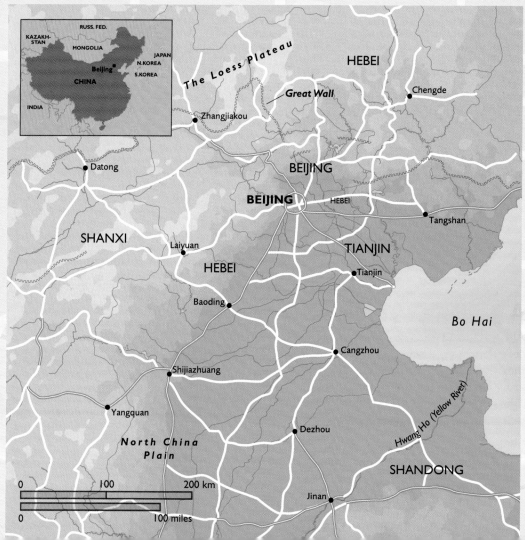

... and opportunity!

Urban centers, particularly major cities, also provide great opportunities for improving life. Cities can provide efficient forms of mass transportation, such as subway or light rail networks. Services such as waste collection, recycling, education, and health care can all work more efficiently in a city. Cities are centers of learning and often the birthplace of new ideas. They provide a platform for arts and culture, and as their populations become more multicultural, these become increasingly global in their nature.

▼ The new Beijing of high-rise towers and increasingly global influences looms large over one of the rapidly disappearing traditional networks of old lanes, or *hutongs*.

A global city

Although all urban centers will share certain things in common, in some cities, the challenges and opportunities facing an urban world are particularly condensed. These are the world's global cities: they reflect the challenges of urbanization, globalization, citizenship, and sustainable development that face us all. Beijing is one of these cities, balancing its role as a city under a secretive and powerful communist government while growing its economy and opening its markets to the world. Beijing is the cultural and political heart of the most populous nation on Earth—its influence is hugely important. This book introduces you to the city and its people, and explores what makes Beijing a truly global city.

Beijing in China

Beijing, located in the middle of flat, dusty north China, was historically a center of power, rather than a commercial city. For centuries, it was closed to foreigners (except invaders) and, as a result, developed more slowly than the international trading cities of Shanghai and Guangzhou (Canton), with their links to Western countries. To China, holding power was always more important than making money. Now, while power is still important, Beijing wants to be rich too.

▶ Wealth and modernity are the important symbols of Beijing today as seen in the densely packed city center viewed from the CCTV tower.

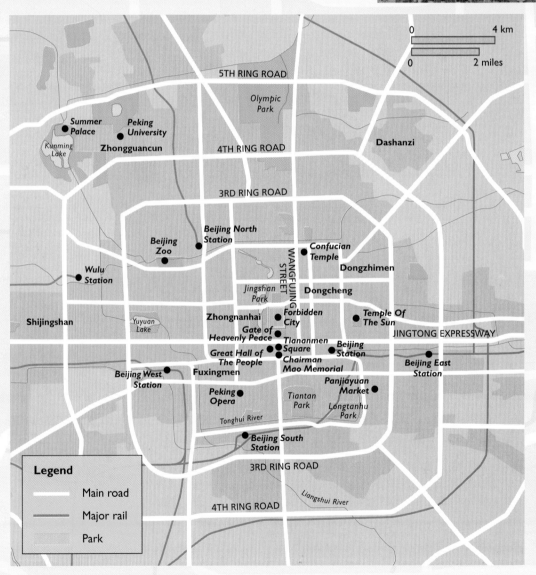

0 ——— 4 km

0 ——— 2 miles

5TH RING ROAD

Olympic Park

Summer Palace

Peking University

Kunming Lake

Zhongguancun

4TH RING ROAD

Dashanzi

3RD RING ROAD

Beijing North Station

Beijing Zoo

Confucian Temple

Dongzhimen

WANGFUJING STREET

Wulu Station

Jingshan Park

Dongcheng

Shijingshan

Yuyuan Lake

Zhongnanhai

Forbidden City

Temple Of The Sun

JINGTONG EXPRESSWAY

Gate of Heavenly Peace

Tiananmen Square

Beijing Station

Great Hall of The People

Chairman Mao Memorial

Beijing East Station

Beijing West Station

Fuxingmen

Panjiayuan Market

Peking Opera

Tiantan Park

Longtanhu Park

Tonghui River

Beijing South Station

3RD RING ROAD

Liangshui River

4TH RING ROAD

Legend

—— Main road

—— Major rail

Park

▲ The center of the city of Beijing.

Local challenge

Beijing's struggle to catch up economically, not only with the Western world, but also with other cities in China, has led to changes at breakneck speed. Like many cities in developing countries, Beijing has grown quickly, creating problems such as pollution, serious water shortages, and traffic. The city has many old buildings but is tearing down its traditional architecture for the sake of modernity. Property developers and business people are getting rich, buying luxury cars and expensive houses, but the homes of many Beijing residents still lack adequate heating or plumbing. There is a significant, visible underclass, riding through the city in mule carts, or piled together in the back of pickup trucks. A shortage of essential resources, an economically divided population, and increasing conflict between traditional values and modern life are all issues facing Beijing in the 21st century.

▲ Beijing sits in the middle of an agricultural area that is rapidly disappearing as the city develops and expands at an incredible rate.

Beijing Facts

Name: Beijing Municipality, one of four municipalities in China (not attached to any province)

Location: North China, surrounded by Hebei Province

Area: 6,490 square miles

Population: 11 million to 15 million, including 3.7 million registered migrants (2005)

County-level divisions: 16 districts, 2 counties

Language: Beijing dialect, basis of standard Mandarin Chinese

The history of Beijing

Beijing has existed as far back as the Zhou Dynasty (1122–221 B.C.E.), when it was a trade outpost for Koreans, Mongols, and tribes from central China. Since then, Beijing has been invaded, flattened, rebuilt, and invaded again, and has served as capital of five different dynasties and of modern day China. The city's history has been a constant struggle between Chinese and foreign elements, or the Chinese against each other.

▶ The Great Wall of China was begun in around 221 B.C.E. to deter invaders from Central Asia from reaching Chinese strongholds, including Beijing, to the south.

Before Beijing

Beijing (then called Ji) was the capital of the Liao (916–1125 C.E.) and Jin Dynasties (1115–1234) of northern China, before Mongol invaders from the north burned it to the ground after a seven-year siege. Ji then became Dadu, the capital of the Mongol Yuan Dynasty (1279–1368), the builders of the famous *hutongs*, or the narrow winding lanes that make up modern Beijing's poorer neighborhoods and are its most popular tourist attractions.

The Yuan Dynasty united China, but financial problems and natural disasters led to its collapse, allowing the Ming Dynasty to return China to Chinese control. Emperor Yong Le designed the modern layout of the city, now renamed Beijing. At the center of Beijing was built the Imperial Palace, or Forbidden City, which was off-limits to the masses. A north-south axis

◀ An elaborately carved walkway in Beijing's Forbidden City. Once strictly off-limits, the Forbidden City is today one off the major tourist attractions in Beijing.

bisects the central area, while the rest of the city is in a grid format, with *hutongs* connecting the main roads.

Beijing (and China) was not in Chinese hands for long. New northern invaders (the Manchus) stormed the capital. The new Manchu Qing Dynasty (1644–1912) expanded Beijing, restored old buildings and constructed new ones—most notably the Summer Palace in the northwest of the city.

Beijing in the 20th century

By the late 19th century, wars and lavish spending by its rulers had weakened the country, allowing foreign powers to establish a military and commercial presence. The Chinese reacted to the unpopular foreign presence with the Boxer Rebellion of 1900. The Boxers were a martial arts group who initially opposed the Qing Dynasty, until they decided foreigners were the greater evil. The Boxers occupied Beijing with over 140,000 soldiers, holding the foreign community hostage for over two months. An alliance of eight foreign powers known as the Eight Power Alliance crushed the rebellion, rescued the hostages, and forced the ruling Dowager Empress Cixi to sign the humiliating Boxer Protocol treaty, which forced the Chinese to pay huge sums in reparations. This treaty is still a source of shame to the Chinese, and is one root of widespread distrust of foreigners today.

▲ Visitors roam among the remains of the first Summer Palace, which was destroyed by French and British troops in the 1860s.

Civil unrest

After the overthrow of the Qing in 1912, warlords overran the capital, and Japanese forces invaded China from the east. In 1918 the government secretly ceded nearby Shandong Province to Japan, and when the treaty became known there were massive student protests. These protests were called the May Fourth Movement (1919), and its leaders established principles of socialism the Chinese Communist Party would later adopt as their own. Without a strong central government, China became prey to competing and violent political groups. The Communist Party of China (CPC), led by Mao Zedong (1893–1976), spent the 1920s and 1930s fighting the right-wing Kuomintang Party (KMT), led by Chiang Kai-shek (1887–1975). When these two groups weren't fighting each other, they fought independent warlords and the Japanese, who, after colonizing northeast China, occupied Beijing in 1937. After the surrender of the Japanese at the end of the Second World War in 1945, the CPC and KMT conflict became known as the Chinese Civil War.

◄ A giant portrait of Mao Zedong, China's most influential communist leader, hangs above Wumen Gate of the Forbidden City.

Mao Zedong

When Mao Zedong's communist Red Army marched through the countryside, he ordered his soldiers not to loot any homes, which helped to recruit a wave of grateful farmers. Mao defeated the KMT with his "peasant revolution" in 1949, and established his capital in Beijing. Over 2 million defeated KMT fled to the island of Taiwan, taking money and cultural treasures with them—which mainlanders still want back. Overseas Chinese returned to the "New China" under Mao, which promised to become a united, prosperous, and peaceful nation. Unfortunately, the next 50 years saw tremendous poverty, and little peace.

In the 1950s the government launched an "anti-rightist campaign" to rid the country of non–Communist Party influences, targeting artists, writers, intellectuals, and wealthy landowners. Following the anti-rightist campaign was the "Great Leap Forward" (1958–60), a program designed to rapidly develop industry and agriculture simultaneously that instead created a nationwide famine between 1960 and 1962 and the death of up to 30 million peasants.

▲ A sculpture at Beijing's National Agricultural Exhibition Center depicts rural workers during the Cultural Revolution era, when farming was an honored profession.

More civil unrest

The next large program introduced by the Communist leadership was called the Cultural Revolution (1966–76), which once again attempted to eradicate China of non-Communist thinking. The professions of soldiers, factory workers, and farmers were honored, while professors, engineers, and scientists were fired, sent to labor camps, imprisoned, or even killed. Beijing's schools, libraries, and universities were closed, and urban teenagers were sent to work on farms, far from the city—sometimes for as long as 10 years.

Other students formed militia groups called Red Guards, each claiming undying loyalty to Mao Zedong. The Red Guards swept through the city, destroying temples and monuments, arresting citizens, confiscating property, and fighting and even killing each other. Neighbors informed on neighbors, students on teachers, and children on parents, and a generation of Chinese grew up without an education. This chaos, lawlessness, and abandonment of traditional values did lasting damage to society.

After Mao

Mao Zedong died in 1976, and the next important leader to follow him was Deng Xiaoping (1904–97), in 1978. Deng reopened the universities and reinstated the dismissed intellectuals and government officials. Most importantly, he gradually changed China to a market economy. The government no longer decided what people could eat, where they could live, or what career they pursued. For the first time making money was allowed, and it became more important than politics.

▼ The gradual opening up of China following Mao's death in 1976 has led to the emergence of wealth as a status symbol.

Massacre

In May 1989, students and workers gathered in Tiananmen Square in central Beijing to protest against government corruption and growing social inequalities. On June 4 the protest was violently crushed by the Chinese military, which killed thousands of protesters—exact figures are not known because the Chinese government will not release them. Horrified foreign nations severed economic and diplomatic ties with China, resulting in a decrease in international trade, investment, and education.

Smaller political protests had occurred before, but the Tiananmen unrest changed how people felt about their government—Beijing residents today have less faith in the government and the Communist Party. The Tiananmen event also taught the Chinese that they were no longer an isolated nation: the world was watching. International opinion suddenly became extremely important to the Chinese, from the authorities down to ordinary citizens. When China joined the World Trade Organization (WTO) in 2000 and Beijing won the right to host the 2008 Olympics, many observers felt that China was being readmitted to international affairs. During the Tang Dynasty (618–907), China was the world leader; now many Chinese feel that China is becoming the leader again.

▼ Tiananmen Square in Beijing has long been a meeting place, but in 1989 a gathering against the government was violently suppressed, earning the square an infamous history.

CASE STUDY

Chen Mei remembers Mao's China

Corporate training consultant Chen Mei was still a child when Mao Zedong died in 1976, but she remembers a different Beijing: blue skies; empty, safe streets; and friendly people. "It has something to do with equality," she says. "Back then, you could be a street sweeper or a university professor, and your lives were the same. Today everyone wants more."

But in those days, people worked together. "My mom was a doctor," Chen says, herself a mother of two. "She used to steal bandages and alcohol, and then swap them with other moms who worked in grocery stores, to get meat or vegetables." In those days, Beijing operated on a rationing system—the government issued tickets for limited supplies of meat, oil, sugar, rice, and other necessities. This was confusing, however, for a child whose teachers kept talking about honesty. "I used

to blame my mom," Chen says, "but I didn't understand life. Foreigners wonder how people survived on seven dollars a year, but that's how we survived. It was a community."

The people of Beijing

As China's capital, and one of its most developed areas, Beijing is a magnet for the rural unemployed and "out-of-province" people who live a semi-legal existence in the city. China has a gigantic population—the same as the United States, Indonesia, Brazil, Pakistan, Bangladesh, Russia, Nigeria, Japan, the United Kingdom, and France combined. A population this big puts massive pressure on natural resources, educational resources, and jobs. This causes resentment among Beijingers toward the rural disadvantaged, who are just looking for a better life.

▲ As Beijing continues to develop, overcrowding, traffic congestion, and air pollution are among the challenges facing the city and its people.

Crowded Beijing

Beijing is China's largest city in area, its municipality measuring 6,490 square miles, just slightly smaller than the state of Kuwait. It has a population density across the entire metropolitan area of 2,311 people per square mile. However, the central area's 7 million live on only 529 square miles, raising the density in the middle of the city to 13,232 people per square mile. Even as the city spreads outward, the center becomes more crowded.

People need places to live, to eat, to work, to relax, and to shop, and the booming construction industry brings money to the local economy. However, many new apartments remain empty, because no one can afford them—yet.

Road traffic is increasing, while clean air and water are rapidly diminishing, and the crowds and noise can be intolerable.

Moving people

Planners are preparing "Beijing 2020"—an 18 million resident megalopolis combining the urban center, suburbs, and 11 satellite cities (see page 57). This will require people to leave their homes as sites are redeveloped. Developers evict some residents under protest or by force; others voluntarily move to find jobs in the high-tech industries, factories, universities, and schools being built in the new cities. Developers are also building luxury apartments in the northern Hui Long Guan and Tian Tong Yuan areas, to lure the wealthy to create affluent suburbs.

The policy was established as a temporary, emergency measure, and today even the tightly controlled official media is suggesting the benefits of a two-child policy instead.

▼ Beijing "in-province" population growth 1950–2015.

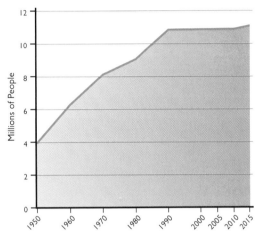

▼ A grandfather cares for his only grandchild on the southern outskirts of the city. The one-child policy dramatically reduced China's population growth, but it may be phased out in the future.

▲ Housing for government workers is demolished in the Sanlitun area to make way for a new development consisting of a shopping center and restaurants.

One-child policy

A controversial consequence of China's staggering population size is the policy established in 1979 that limits couples to one child. Since the founding of "New China" (the People's Republic of China) in 1949, the population has increased by around 700 million. The policy is an attempt to arrest this huge growth in population. It applies only to the majority urban Han Chinese, but not to rural Chinese, ethnic minorities (China has 56 ethnic groups), couples where both partners were only children, or those married to foreigners.

The "out of Beijing" population

Beijing has a large migrant population, but rather than having migrants from abroad, as in many other global cities, migrants in Beijing come from within China. Some of these migrants are from ethnic minorities and some from the majority Han Chinese.

▲ Migrant workers carrying their possessions in tarpaulin bags arrive at the Dongzhimen bus station. Many rural migrants arrive in Beijing in this way, hoping to find work.

Hukous

Before potential migrants can move around China they need a *hukou*, or residency permit. Beijing is very attractive to migrants for its educational and job opportunities, even if taking up those opportunities means leaving families behind. For this reason the city government makes it hard for outer-province students to get *hukous* and attend universities in Beijing; the government's view is that after they graduate, they will add to the city's permanent population.

Getting a *hukou* is not a guarantee of finding work, and well-paid jobs may be hard to find. In order to prevent out-of-work migrants causing trouble, the Beijing authorities try to find the new migrants

▲ A resident shows his *hukou*, or residency permit—the pass necessary to access almost anything in Beijing.

work of any kind, no matter how trivial. As a result, many people get jobs that seem pointless: bored subway attendants rip passenger tickets, and throw both halves away; office supply stores have different clerks for pens, paper, and notebooks (shoppers have to bring their receipts to the cash register and then go back to collect their purchase); and security guards are everywhere, guarding nothing.

Life of migrants

The newspaper *China Daily* puts Beijing's average salary at US$466 per month; Beijingers claim it's about US$248. Unskilled migrant workers, such as wait staff and construction workers, can expect to earn as little as US$30–60 monthly— low by the standards of ordinary Beijingers, but higher than in the migrants' home provinces. Many low-salary workers live in military-style dormitories or tarpaulin tents and have little access to medical care or education. Construction workers are usually only paid once a year before the Chinese New Year, when they traditionally travel back to their homes. Sometimes crooked bosses run away with the money before payday, leaving the workers penniless, but the government is cracking down on such practices.

Hundreds of thousands of Koreans, Europeans, and North Americans study or work in Beijing. Beijingers often resent the disproportionately high wages these people earn but feel that English teachers and international business people will help China's development.

▶ Migrant construction workers from Henan Province in their sleeping and living quarters. These men have been hired to build the stadium that will hold the Olympics in Beijing in 2008.

While all of China's 56 ethnic groups are represented in Beijing, the following 10 groups have the largest membership.

Ethnic Group Breakdown in Beijing, according to 2000 Census

Group (nationality)	Number	Percentage
Han Chinese	12,983,696	95.69
Manchu	250,286	1.84
Hui	235,837	1.74
Mongol	37,464	0.28
Korean / Chinese	20,369	0.15
Tujia	8,372	0.062
Zhuang	7,322	0.054
Miao	5,291	0.039
Uyghur	3,129	0.023
Tibetan	2,920	0.022

Living in the city

With its 11 million to 15 million people, Beijing is China's second largest city, after Shanghai. Most of the population is from the ethnic Han majority group, but small pockets of ethnic minorities exist. With its strong central government and position as China's most important cultural and political center, Beijing has had investment in health care and education, but with its huge growth in population in the last 50 years the pressures on such services have become almost intolerable.

▶ The outpatient department of the Peking Union Hospital.

Health care

Hospitals in Beijing are better than almost anywhere else in China, and many Western-style facilities meet international standards, but health care is expensive. Doctors are underpaid and unsatisfied, and the hospitals are very crowded.

Government and multinational company employees get some reimbursement for medical bills, but actual health insurance is nonexistent. Patients must bring cash deposits equivalent to over US$1,000 to secure hospital treatment, even for emergency care. This is one reason why China has a personal savings rate of about 40 percent of income, compared to 1 percent in the United States.

Another problem is the lack of primary care: sometimes patients needing non-emergency care must have *guanxi* (connections) to see a doctor at all. By developing country standards, Beijing does have a high rate of doctors to patients—1.6 per 1,000 (India only has 0.4 per 1,000), but China as a whole needs a half million new doctors to bring services up to a Western standard. Doctors are well respected but they must work long, high-pressure hours for low pay. Surgeons are the best-paid doctors, but they earn only about US$700 a month—including bribes from the patients' families. Foreign English language teachers working half the hours earn twice as much money. Many disgusted doctors are leaving the profession, preferring to work in medical supply sales, patent offices, or even the travel industry.

▲ Prescriptions for traditional Chinese medicines are carefully weighed out in a Beijing hospital. Herbal remedies continue to play a major role in Chinese health care.

▲ Medical staff discuss patient care at the Bayley & Jackson Medical Center, a private health care clinic that mainly caters to the expatriate community.

SARS

The severe acute respiratory syndrome (SARS) outbreak of 2003 originated in southern China. Quickly carried around the world by air transportation, this new illness caused deaths in Singapore, Hong Kong, Vietnam, and Canada. As the transportation hub of China, Beijing was hit especially hard. SARS was carried in by migrant workers and spread through the city. Residents resorted to wearing face masks and boiling vinegar to purify the air. Schools closed; restaurants were deserted; and checkpoints to test people's body temperature were set up outside buildings and on highways. Precise statistics are unavailable, but hundreds of Chinese died and thousands were infected.

The city authorities were accused of covering up the extent of the problem, but since then important lessons have been learned: that disease spreads rapidly through a country of 1.3 billion people, that secrecy damages credibility, and that epidemics harm the national economy—the tourism industry lost US$2.4 billion in two months. Learning from SARS, China has adopted aggressive policies for dealing with HIV/AIDS, involving education programs, free testing, and even needle exchange.

▶ A pedestrian considers an HIV/AIDS awareness poster in a subway passage.

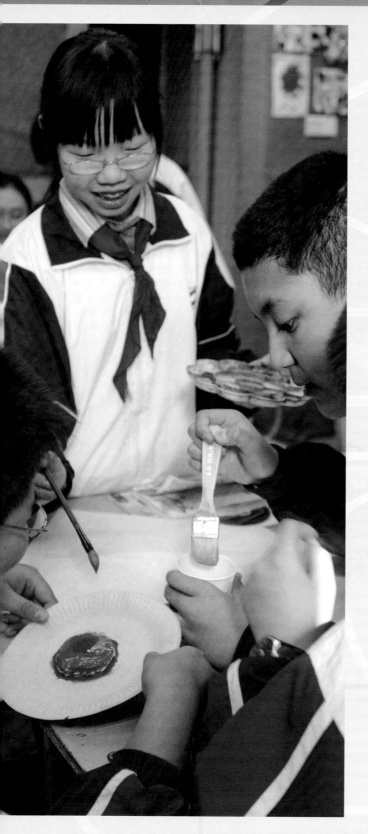

Education

Beijing schools use a system of learning based on rote memorization, where authority is unquestioned. This results in millions of students who struggle to express their opinions. This hurts Chinese working in international companies and even in China, because students do not develop creativity and problem-solving skills.

School classes can have between 40 and 60 students, which makes it hard for teachers to give individual attention where it is needed. Teachers are often blamed for poor student performance, so they often try to raise standards by shaming underperforming children. Primary school goes from age six to 12, middle school from 13 to 15, and high school from 16 to 18, with entrance exams at every level. Students can win academic or athletic scholarships to the better out-of-district schools. In addition to the 251-day school year (the world's longest), most take *ke wai*—extra weekend or off-season classes. These and school fees make the "free" education very expensive—many parents say they couldn't afford more than one child, even if there weren't a one-child policy.

Beijing students tend to stay in the same group of classmates for years, so they often form close relationships that continue long after graduation and may even help future job opportunities. Students also develop emotional security—there are few problems with bullying in Beijing schools.

◀ Students enjoy an art class at a middle school in Dongzhimen.

The *gao kao*

Students at the top schools can better prepare for the *gao kao*, or university entrance exam, the result of which determines their university, course of study, and future job success. A child in a good university can mean financial security for the family, so studying is a group effort. Parents sometimes give up their jobs to monitor their children's progress; grandparents may attend classes, sneaking in tape recorders or taking notes. Some children breathe in pure oxygen (from special "oxygen bars") for energy; the parents of others rent homes closer to school. The Beijing government stops construction near testing centers months before the exam, and parents lobby their apartment complexes to stop excess noise.

The *gao kao*, besides adding pressure to the lives of students, also prevents education reform. The government does try to free teachers from the rigid curriculum and encourage more classroom "democracy," but parents worry so much about *gao kao* results that the system is hard to change. One advantage of the system is its legitimacy—in a city where street vendors sell university diplomas outside train stations, the *gao kao* is a more valid sign of academic achievement.

▲ A student checks notice boards at the Peking University campus. Peking University is Beijing's premier university and admission is highly prized.

Preserving old Beijing

In the past Beijing was a flat city with one-story courtyard housing called *siheyuans*, along winding *hutongs* (lanes). Some *siheyuans* are over 800 years old; most lack kitchens, bathrooms, and central heating, and their coal stoves make Beijing's pollution even worse. Despite their often primitive living conditions, however, many people consider them the heart of the city. Unfortunately their central location is ideal

▲ The remains of a demolished *hutong* with a tree standing in what would have been the courtyard. Many of the *hutongs* in Beijing have met a similar fate in the name of modernization and development.

for the building of high-priced apartments, and tearing them down is easier than preserving them for the future.

Some feel that the houses are no longer fit for habitation, but residents claim they can be renovated for as little as US$3,000. Unfortunately, Mao's land redistribution programs destroyed all records of their ownership, leaving *hutong* dwellers locked in uncertain legal battles with aggressive and well-funded developers.

◀ Tourism could be the savior of the *hutong* in Beijing. This *hutong* has been converted from a residence to a restaurant. Others have become trendy bars.

Hutong life

Hutongs foster good citizenship in a way impersonal high-rise buildings cannot, as residents meet each other in the course of their day. Residents run dry cleaning or tailoring services or even small restaurants out of their homes—relocating means a loss of livelihood as well as community. Children play in the quiet streets away from traffic, and the elderly get the social contact they need. Even young professionals feel insulated from Beijing's chaos. The Beijing authorities are experimenting with solutions, such as encouraging local government and residents to work together in creating an economically sustainable neighborhood.

▲ Beijing's *hutongs* are a stark contrast to the congestion, noise, and pollution of the modern city and provide for a better quality of community life.

CASE STUDY

Ding Ai, *hutong* preservation activist

"How will we know where we came from?" asks Ding Ai, a *hutong* preservation activist. "You know you came from your mother, and she came from her mother. If we destroy the city's history, how will we know where we came from?" When Ding found her house branded with the character *chai* (destroy), she sprang into action. Knowing she had only 30 days to vacate her family home, she hired architects and engineers who submitted affidavits, swearing to its structural integrity, then she promised to renovate. She succeeded in saving her home.

Now Ding wants to save the city. "Everything in the old city is gold," she says. "And the area is so small already, why do they have to make it smaller?" She campaigns for clearer property laws, lobbies to protect historical areas, and writes articles for newspapers and journals. "Foreigners don't want to fly on a plane for

15 hours to see tall buildings; they can see them at home," she scoffs. "Without the *hutongs*, it's not Beijing." She acknowledges that the government is working on solutions but points out that people move faster than laws. "*Hutongs* get torn down every day," she says sadly. "There's no time."

The survival of tradition

China's long history has created a tradition of spectacular and unusual crafts, and craftspeople continue work their families have done for generations. But China's fascination with rapid development and conspicuous consumption has would-be artisans choosing careers in engineering or information technology, and traditional crafts are struggling to survive.

▼ High-tech skills such as computer engineering are in much greater demand by today's youth than traditional skills.

Chinese claim to be very proud of their craft history but choose to spend their money on computer games, iPods, or new cars instead, leaving these multi-generational craftspeople struggling. Another problem is that during the Cultural Revolution, all traditional activities were prohibited, and a whole generation of parents never taught their children about their history. Some Beijingers are starting culture schools, hoping Chinese will learn their own cultural traditions and teach foreigners in Beijing. Others hope that government will give tax breaks or subsidies to artists preserving China's culture, but this seems unlikely in the near future. Like *hutongs* and *siheyuans*, traditional crafts have to depend on the tourist trade and foreign interest.

▼ Modern global brands and growing consumerism threaten the survival of many traditional crafts and industries in Beijing.

Crafts

Skilled craftspeople carve elaborate sculpture using ice (*bingdiao*), dough (*miansu*), or even butter (*suyouhua*). Hair embroidery (*faxiu*) is especially difficult, since hair is more brittle than silk. Microscopic carving (*weidao*) is usually done on ivory or a single strand of human hair—artisans must feel with their fingers only. Shanghai's Zhang Yunhu reproduced the entire Communist Party of China Constitution (14,000 characters) on a chip of ivory only 1.1 square inches, about the size of a postage stamp. The text is visible only under 100x magnification.

Tang Yujie, crafts maker

"Every country has its good points," says Tang Yujie, owner of Bannerman Tang's Toys and Handicrafts. "Western countries have developed technology; China has a traditional culture. I want the world to know the real China." The Tang family is descended from high-level Qing Dynasty officials and has been

making traditional crafts for five generations. Tang's father taught his wife and children how to make his family's crafts; they worked nights making the pieces he sold at temple fairs and markets. Four years ago, 38-year old Tang left an accounting job to open her own traditional craft shop—a risky proposition in a country obsessed with financial security, but Tang felt she had no choice. "I wanted to continue my father's work," she says. The Tang crafts are original and handmade, and unique to her family. "I also want young Chinese people to learn about culture." Chinese youth measure a nation's success by its economic development and feel embarrassed at China's poverty, a fact that Tang finds upsetting. "China is not poor in money," she says firmly. "China is only poor in spirit." And she knows if Beijing wants to show the world the "best Olympics yet," Beijingers must know something about their past.

The Beijing economy

Overseas investment in China's economy has driven it from global insignificance to the world's fourth largest in just 25 years, with an annual growth rate of 9.9 percent in 2005 (the U.S. rate was 3.5 percent). Beijing accounts for 3.1 percent (US$51.4 billion) of this growth; this investment in the capital city means more manufacturing and increased investment in the city infrastructure, high-tech industries, and large scale environmental projects.

▶ The China World Trade Center building is symbolic of the expansion in international trade for both Beijing and China.

China's trade

China's 1.3 billion people compose both the world's largest single market and the planet's cheapest labor force. Foreign companies relocate their factories, pay less for workers and materials, and sell their goods for a higher profit back home. The Chinese want to be more than the world's factory, however. By insisting that foreign and Chinese companies work in joint ventures, they ensure China develops to fully compete in a globalized world.

◀ China's is the world's largest consumer market but wages are so low that few can afford to shop in luxury malls such as this.

▼ Contribution to Beijing's economy by sector.

Manufacturing 26%

Services 62.4%

Financial 11.6%

Beijing's industries

Foreign investors appreciate Beijing's reputation for safety and stability, as well as the rapid development and the international credibility the 2008 Olympics has created. Today, multinational corporations establish both regional headquarters and research and development (R&D) centers in special economic zones, such as Central Business District (CBD) and Finance Street. Zhongguancun, which is Beijing's Silicon Valley and its brightest economic star, is home to 8,000 high-tech industries, and Microsoft and Motorola are among the 20-plus multinationals to establish R&D centers there.

Manufacturing is still Beijing's largest single industry, providing 88.6 percent of its total industrial output value. Beijing is also expanding its auto industry, which is located in outlying suburban districts such as Tongzhou, Miyun, and Huairou.

▲ The foreign director of an animal feed factory meets Chinese businessmen at a sales conference on the outskirts of Huairou district in Beijing. International partnerships are an important aspect of Beijing's economic growth.

CASE STUDY

Shaan Price, party organizer

Since coming to Beijing from the United States, Shaan Price has modeled, taught English, worked for both UNESCO and an import-export company, and played a large role in the film *Muo Gong*, or *Battle of Wits*. But parties are what come naturally. "It started as just a way to get all my Chinese and foreign friends together," he says of his first nightclub-sized birthday event, "and I wanted to raise money for a local orphanage." His guests never knew that their drinks paid for an orphan's cleft-palate surgery.

The owners of a local nightclub were impressed by Price's social contacts and offered him a partnership in exchange for his design and business ideas. But business relationships with Chinese can be challenging. "There is little trust of foreigners, or even other Chinese," he explains. "And the drive for money is so strong, you can feel it." As for success in Beijing, he says, "You need a creative eye, and the drive to try something new."

Government work

In 1978, Deng Xiaoping said, "To get rich is glorious." His words turned an enormous socialist economy upside down. During Mao's time, private enterprise had been illegal, and everyone worked for the State. *Danweis*, or work units, provided workers with their food, clothing, housing, work, and pensions, as well as controlling their personal lives—marriage, divorce, and even childbirth. *Danweis* still nominally exist, but gone are the guaranteed jobs and benefits of the State Owned Enterprise (SOE) system. Today's Chinese must learn to provide for themselves.

Unemployment

Drastically slashing the SOE workforce helped Beijing's sluggish economy, but it left many middle-aged workers without work. Having grown up during the Cultural Revolution, they lacked the skills and education to be competitive. Beijing's official unemployment level hovers at 2.5 percent, but the real number is probably higher. Educated Beijingers feel government jobs are boring and poorly paid, with advancement impossible without proper *guanxi* (connections). Most want to work abroad, or for multinational joint-ventures, where connections aren't important and the pay is better.

▼ Government employees collect tickets on the Beijing subway. Where once everyone worked for the government, private employment is becoming the norm today.

Bilingual Beijing

This globalization of Beijing has created another sector of the economy—Teaching English as a Foreign Language, or TEFL. Having an English-speaking Beijing workforce means the high-priced foreigners would no longer be needed, leaving more international companies in local hands. A bilingual Beijing is also a viable alternative to Indian cities for Western outsourcing of industries like call centers. Beijingers can learn Western medical, technological, research, and management techniques abroad. The ones who stay away send back money; others, called *hai gui* (sea turtles), return home to make the most of their new skills in the growing economy.

The upcoming 2008 Beijing Olympics is an important catalyst for English education. The Beijing Organizing Committee of the Olympic Games (BOCOG) has plans for the "Best Olympics in World History" that go beyond traffic management or stadium construction to bilingual volunteers. "To foreigners, you represent China," says the directive; "to Chinese you represent Beijing." Even taxi drivers are supposed to be studying from their "taxi English" book, though drivers rarely have the courage to practice with foreigners.

▲ Students practice their English conversation at one of the many language schools in Beijing. The ability to speak English is considered essential to career success, particularly among younger people.

Informal economy

Of course, not every worker needs English. Beijing also has an extensive informal economy, made up of "out of Beijing" people. Every neighborhood has bicycle repairmen, tailors, cobblers, and key makers who work on the sidewalks, and fruit vendors who sell out of mule carts. Recyclers sift through garbage bins for cardboard or bottles, or steal metal manhole covers from the street. Vendors squat on pedestrian bridges selling jewelry, hair clips, stolen books, and fake telephone cards. And pirated DVDs are everywhere—on sidewalks, in black canvas bags, and in small, clearly labeled shops—for sale at US$1 for a movie, US$8 for a whole television series.

▼ A man waits for passing trade at his mobile key cutting and bicycle repair workshop. Such enterprises are a familiar part of Beijing's informal economy.

▲ The main Olympic stadium for the 2008 games under construction in 2006. The Olympics have led to a massive construction boom in the city.

Urban renewal

The 2008 Olympics' massive construction boom is giving rise to stadiums, apartment complexes, and even a National Theater. Beijing's urban renewal is visible everywhere. Places like Sanlitun and Houhai were low-income residential areas that have changed into fashionable nightspots.

Even south Beijing, usually dismissed as "poor," is attracting a class of young, upwardly mobile Chinese. But the most dramatic shift in land use has seen abandoned military factories turned into centers for the creation and sale of contemporary art by local Chinese artists.

▲ "Photo 798" is one of the art galleries that has contributed to the regeneration of Dashanzi, a former industrial area of Beijing.

Factory galleries

After the military abandoned the buildings, the high-ceilinged ex-factories of places like Dashanzi, with their large windows and natural light were perfect for Beijing's fledgling art community. Foreign collectors have paid as much as US$412,775 for contemporary Chinese works. With the art gallery boom came coffee shops, restaurants, and offices for designers and publishers.

Poor artists have a way of creating trendy neighborhoods. Dashanzi is no exception, except with one Chinese twist—this area has become so valuable, it's now threatened with demolition. Dashanzi straddles the corridor between the city and the airport, making it an ideal place for luxury high-rises or an expansion of Zhongguancun. Artists have successfully petitioned to preserve the area until after the Olympics, but once the games are over no one knows what will happen.

Many feel that creative zones like Dashanzi are important to a city that wants to evolve beyond being a global manufacturing center. Another important issue is intellectual property: China is notorious for copying, pirating, or counterfeiting design ideas and products from other countries. It may only stop when its own inventions and products are threatened.

CASE STUDY

Song Zhuang, an artist community

In 1995, a group of ten artists clustered in hovels around Yuanmingyuan, the ruins of the first Summer Palace, before they were driven out. Today, those ten artists have evolved into Song Zhuang, the world's largest art community, with 500 artists living in villages just outside Dashanzi. "Back then, the government control over art was very tight," says Sally Liu, owner of the Artist Village Gallery. "You couldn't have an exhibition—the police would come and shut it down. But today, the government gets financial benefit from this community." When Liu took a neighborhood landfill and turned it into a successful gallery, she tripled the property values of the neighboring homes.

"It's the most active group for experimental art," says Liu, "and the only one with such a long history." Artists come from all over China, attracted by the fame of former Song Zhuang members that have become art celebrities. But Sally Liu doesn't think about fame. "I try to help those who are not famous, but who are very talented," says Liu. "Emerging artists."

▶ An artist at work in the Song Zhuang community.

Managing Beijing

China's 3.7 million square miles is divided into various zones of government—there are 22 provinces, five Autonomous Regions, and two Special Autonomous Regions, with an average population of 45.3 million each. Beijing, however, is one of China's four municipalities—cities under central government control (the others are Shanghai, Chongqing, and Tianjin). As China's seat of national government, Beijing has some special challenges.

The Beijing municipal government

The Beijing municipal government controls China's largest city by area. Beijing is composed of two counties and 16 districts—four urban, four suburban, and eight outlying suburban districts. The city government's six major departments oversee such functions as education, economics and development, science and technology, and ethnic and minority affairs, as well as security and general administration.

▲ A police officer checks the papers of a street trader in front of the Forbidden City.

Law enforcement

The most visible law enforcement department is the Public Security Bureau (PSB), essentially Beijing's police force. However, besides dealing with criminals, riots, prisons, and traffic safety, the PSB handles firefighting, provides security to government agencies and visiting guests of the state, and overseas travel and residency affairs for citizens, migrants, and foreigners. The PSB also must "have full knowledge of the elements affecting policy stability, harming domestic security and disrupting public order." Secret groups are automatically suspect in China—for example, although Beijing has plenty of churches, Christian groups meeting at private homes may have been visited by the PSB. Citizens have the right to belong to a religion, but it must be officially sanctioned.

▲ An officer in the Beijing Fire Department demonstrates equipment at a presentation held at the Forbidden City to encourage public awareness in fire safety.

The Communist Party of China (CPC)

At one time, the Communist Party controlled people's work, homes, marriage, children, and success. Outstanding elementary school students became Young Pioneers; studious teenagers joined the Youth League; and 18 year olds joined the Party—if they knew the right people. The Party was the fast track to a better life.

Although the CPC ranks are still growing, joining today offers fewer immediate benefits, and people's loyalty is to their families and their country before the Party. Even government itself is less about ideology and more about removing obstacles to rapid development.

Since different police officers and judges will state different regulations in their dealings with people, the first step for the Beijing authorities has been to attempt to create a uniform set of laws that everyone can recognize. China's reputation for corruption and producing counterfeit goods makes doing international business hard, so the authorities are now ordering more high-profile arrests of corrupt officials. Civil rights are also improving; there are more discrimination and personal injury lawsuits passing through the courts, and more patent lawyers are protecting intellectual property.

Lei Feng

Before Deng Xiaoping's reforms, a good grasp of party ideology was important for personal advancement. The folk hero Lei Feng—a brave, self-sacrificing peasant—was held up as an example; today students still "learn from Lei Feng." "Capitalist" business leaders were allowed to join the CPC only in 2002. Today, individual Beijingers control their own personal and professional lives, and even government officials can be non-Party members. Children still join the Young Pioneers and the Youth League and do volunteer work on March 5, Lei Feng Day, but these organizations are not as important as they used to be.

▼ The badge of the Mao Youth League is one use of symbolism in China's giant communist party propaganda, though today the CPC is less influential in everyday lives.

▲ Gateway leading to the offices of the Mayor of Beijing. Like much of government in China, the political offices of Beijing are shrouded in secrecy and security is always high.

Citizenship

Beijing's Mayor and nine Vice Mayors are elected in five-year terms. In addition Beijing has 4,403 deputies, elected in five-year terms by the city's 2,336 electoral wards. But the word "elections" can be misleading. Few non-Party candidates are allowed to run for even lower office—many who try are hindered by unhelpful bureaucrats and mountains of red tape. Beijing has an official 95 percent voter turnout rate, but in fact no one actually seems to vote. There is little to choose between candidates up for election. However, Beijing and the rest of China are experimenting with democracy. Residents' Committees (RCs) used to serve the residents of small areas, but were viewed by most people with suspicion as "thought police." Today, however, with more unemployment and fewer state services, people are looking for help. RCs are expanding their territories, from hundreds to thousands of households—and as more homes are threatened with destruction, more locals are using RCs to demand their rights as citizens.

◀ A community leader, signified by the red arm band, helps connect the local government and the community for which she is responsible.

Volunteerism

Volunteer work is new to China. Taking care of families was difficult enough, so helping strangers seemed ridiculous. But families can only do so much, and nowadays, the state does less than ever. Wang Xingjuan started one of China's first nongovernmental organizations (NGOs), located in Beijing—the Maple Women's Psychological Counseling Center. The center helps victims of domestic violence and runs a suicide hotline—Chinese women are at particularly high risk. Other volunteer-run organizations in Beijing include Friends of Nature and Global Village Beijing, which work to raise awareness of the city's severe environmental problems (see page 50); Hua Dan, a theater group that helps migrant workers to improve their self-esteem; and Magic Hospital, which provides free entertainment in the Children's Hospital. Groups like these have started to show Beijingers how volunteer work can benefit their communities, without the involvement of the city or national authorities.

▼ A passerby reads a board appealing for blood donors. Volunteering is a relatively new concept in China.

National government

Tiananmen Square is home to China's most important buildings: The Forbidden City, Mao Zedong's Mausoleum, and the Great Hall of the People, the seat of the national legislature. Little information is available on what happens inside the Great Hall, but it is here that the laws of the nation are made. Officially, the Communist Party of China (CPC) and the government are two separate entities, but in practice there is little meaningful difference. Some national leaders have had different titles—Party Chairman, General Secretary, or President. For some time Deng Xiaoping's only title, despite being the unquestioned leader of China, was Honorary Chairman of the Chinese Contract Bridge Association! Currently, the leadership is divided under three titles: General Secretary of the Party, President of China, and Chairman of the Central Military Commission—and one leader does not necessarily hold all offices. Despite the mystery, however, Beijing citizens love to talk politics.

▼ The Great Hall of the People is the seat of the Chinese government.

Transportation for Beijing

While Beijing is well linked to large national and international cities, local transportation services within the city are struggling to keep pace with the city's rapid development. Many residents have turned to the car as an alternative to public transportation or the traditional bicycle, creating huge congestion and pollution problems.

▲ Passengers disembark from a regional airline. Domestic air travel is growing rapidly in China, and Beijing is a key hub in this network.

National links

An inland city, Beijing has no port but shares port services with the neighboring city of Tianjin, another municipality, about 85 miles to the east. The port handles 75 million tons of goods annually. Beijing is the center of the national railroad network, which is continuing to expand. On July 1, 2006, a luxury train route from Beijing to Tibet opened, and authorities are planning

▼ New trains are part of a massive investment in local and national rail services for Beijing and beyond.

a high-speed train to Shanghai. The city's new airport, due for completion by 2008, is said to be the world's largest. Beijing plans to open a second airport in 2010, this time in the underdeveloped southern area of the city.

Traffic

Car and traffic congestion has become an enormous problem in Beijing in a very short span of time. Beijing issues 2,000 new license plates daily—as many as Shanghai issues in a month. The 2 million cars on Beijing's roads in 2006 were seven years ahead of projections; current projections predict 3.5 million for 2008. Economically this is a good thing—for every one car sold, two jobs are created. But as car use increases 10 percent annually, road capacity is increasing by only 2 percent. Today, just less than 30 percent of Beijingers use the subway, which, with only three lines, does not have nearly enough capacity. Most major cities with subways share problems of capacity shortage, and that is one reason that private vehicle use is increasing in cities like Beijing. Eight planned additional lines should ease the burden on the existing network and take some traffic off the roads as the drivers return to public transportation. The government is also increasing urban and suburban rail capacity and building more highways and parallel roads. Officials are also discussing a possible congestion tax, and a higher parking fee, up from the current US$0.12 per hour.

▶ Road traffic is becoming a major problem in Beijing, especially during rush hour when even major new roads with multiple lanes can grind to a halt.

CASE STUDY

Kong Fangchang, taxi driver

Kong Fangchang found taxi driving a welcome change from the monotony of a government electrician's job, but after 12 years, things are different: traffic levels have risen enormously. "It's rush hour all day long," says Fangchang. Gas prices have almost doubled, and the fleet of new taxis that the authorities say the drivers must use cost more to repair.

Another problem is the explosion of *hei che*, or illegal unlicensed taxis. Once a feature of only the remotest suburbs, these taxis have come into central areas. "Illegal taxis can wait in the areas taxis aren't allowed," says Fangchang, "and the police don't notice them. There's

only so much business out there, and they are getting a big piece of the pie." The rise in the number of illegal taxis and private cars also means fewer people hailing taxis from the side of the road. As a consequence Fangchang's monthly income of US$248 keeps shrinking.

▲ Bicycles remain a popular mode of travel here during the morning rush hour, but the car is being given priority in many parts of the city because it is considered more "modern."

Car alternatives

Despite manufacturing more and more cars, China remains the world leader in bicycle production, making over 60 million annually. For most of the 20th century Beijing was a city of bicycles, with millions using this healthy and environmentally safe form of transportation. A popular innovation is the electric bicycle, which became illegal in January 2006 (but is still used). Beijing's government claimed the electric bicycles were unsafe, but according to critics, officials feel that cars will better boost Beijing's "developed city" image.

Transportation alternatives

Beijing's informal transportation economy is based on illegal taxis and motorcycles waiting for fares outside subway stations and in outlying neighborhoods. More common are the *san lun che* (three-wheeled vehicles) for transporting either goods or people. These can be pedicabs, pulled by bicycles or mopeds, or open carts attached to "tricycles." Mule-drawn carts can be used to haul bricks at construction sites, or fruit around neighborhoods.

The bicycle culture

Bicycle safety equipment, while readily available, is rarely used, despite the heavy car traffic on the roads. Whole families can be seen weaving through traffic perched on a single bicycle with no light, one reflector, and a tiny bell. Cyclists seem more worried about weather than traffic, frequently wearing special gear to block sandstorms or sunlight. Good locks are important, however, as bicycle theft is common. Some riders pay "bike watchers" outside shops to stand guard while they are inside, or buy very cheap bicycles that can be easily replaced. A popular bicycle is the steel Fei Ge (Flying Pigeon). Status symbols when they first appeared in the 1960s, they are still used today, but more modern racing and mountain bikes are used by wealthier Chinese.

▲ A bicycle watcher at a parking area for bikes outside a subway station.

CASE STUDY

Beijing for Bikes (B4B)

Many Chinese think that a first class city means cars and that bicycles make the city look poor. At the same time they complain about pollution and traffic. Friends of Nature's Beijing for Bikes (B4B) initiative is trying to promote cycling as a healthy, sustainable transportation option, not an economic necessity. "Over half our pollution comes from our 2 million cars," says Hu Huizhe, director of B4B.

Beijing has wide, flat streets that form a city grid and have bicycle lanes separated by a tree barrier—the perfect infrastructure for a cycling city. But as roads are widened to allow more car traffic, bicycle lanes get removed. Hu Huizhe organizes bicycle publicity and awareness events, and campaigns for car-free zones in Beijing. "By 2008, traffic will be a big problem," Huizhe says, "and if we want to welcome guests from all over the world [for the Olympic Games], we have to make space for them."

Culture, leisure, and tourism

Beijing is China's tourist capital. As the seat of power, the city has great appeal for many Chinese. For foreigners, Beijing combines a modern, diverse, international city with most of China's greatest cultural treasures.

The heart of the city

Tiananmen (Gate of Heavenly Peace) has been the spiritual center of Beijing, and all China, since 1417, but it was Mao who built the world's largest public square, measuring 100 acres, the size of 130 football fields. Beijingers congregate there to picnic and fly kites, even in winter, and foreigners visit because of its history. To the north of the square is the Forbidden City. Built in 1406, these 800 buildings with 9,000 rooms cover 250 acres, or nearly nine times as much surface area as the Pentagon. Other popular places outside the Forbidden City include the architecturally stunning Temple of Heaven, completed in 1420, which was a place where the emperor prayed for good harvests, and the Summer Palace to the northwest of the city, which surrounds an enormous lake where boating trips are popular in the summer.

▼ Huang Qiong Yu (the Imperial Vault of Heaven), part of Tiantan Gongyuan (the Temple of Heaven complex).

Other attractions

Just north of Beijing is the famous Great Wall (see page 8). Construction and repair have been piecemeal over about 2,000 years, but it was during the Ming Dynasty (1368–1644) that most of the sections were joined and the wall assumed the form we know today. Built with brick, egg yolk, and rice paste as a way to keep northern invaders out, it proved ineffective as protection, and isolated China from the world, which hindered its development. Today the parts of the Wall easily accessed from Beijing are a huge tourist draw, but visitors can also see the "Wild Wall" in Beijing's suburbs. This is the unpaved Great Wall, with crumbling brick surrounded by silent forests. In summer, foreigners camp (illegally) in the guard towers, paying local villagers to deliver firewood and beer.

Many visitors to Beijing go to some of the local markets. Panjiaoyuan is 3,000 stalls of (mostly fake) antiques, while the Ya Show and Xiu Shui markets have rows of cheap clothing, jewelry, and souvenirs.

Beijing has many popular shows, such as Chinese Acrobats, Kung Fu, or Jingju (Peking Opera), a 200-year-old art form where storytelling combines speaking, singing, martial arts, and elaborate makeup. More modern entertainment is also widely available, with bands and DJs to be seen in clubs and at music festivals. There is also a Beijing punk movement, and the contemporary art scene (see page 35) is becoming more popular every passing year.

▲ A trader reaches for a porcelain vase to show a customer at the "antique market" at Panjiaoyuan, east of the city center.

▶ Followers of the Beijing punk movement.

Sports and leisure

For a city with such stifling air pollution and notoriously bad weather, Beijing has a great deal of outdoor activity. The Chinese believe in taking physical exercise to maintain balance (known as *yin* and *yang*). Beijing families go hiking in the mountains, and boating or swimming illegally in city lakes. Many residential areas have playgrounds in public places. Basketball is very popular—most Chinese boys believe playing basketball will make them taller. Running is rare, but badminton and jump rope are very popular.

Other, less strenuous activities include playing Chinese chess on street corners and *wei qi* (the game known as *go* in Japan) in teahouses. Some people do *tai chi* or traditional fan dances in the parks.

Beijing's growing middle class is interested less in *tai chi*, and more in golf, scuba diving, and flying lessons. At a nearby reservoir, city-dwellers do weekend paragliding off surrounding hills, while not far away, shepherds look after their flocks. Wealthier and younger Chinese are more

▲ Kite flying is a popular activity. On the bridge that spans Kunming Lake at the Summer Palace, a kite flyer launches his butterfly kites into the blue sky.

conscious of their physical appearance than their health, and may exercise to maintain their weight, not "balance."

▼ Fan dancers in Ri Tan Park.

Organized sports

Beijing's dense population and limited space mean there are few community sports organizations. Coaches do recruit school children for teams; interested students attend training centers for swimming, gymnastics, table tennis, or other sports. The best athletes may eventually join national or army teams, and for poorer children this may provide a route to a free education.

▶ Talent is often spotted early and the best athletes receive strong encouragement from the authorities.

CASE STUDY

Yang Hong Jin, Ambassador of Athletics

As Program Director of the Beijing International Sports Center, former weightlifter Yang Hong Jin organizes sports exchanges between amateur Chinese and Western teams. Athletes get to enjoy sightseeing and friendly competition, and learn about cultural differences. "China and America have different training systems," Yang says. "In China, the children are selected at a very young age, and training is free. But then they get lazy. In America they have to pay for training," he continues, "so they want to do it."

Leisure sports have a very short history in China; even in the 1980s, training was for competition only. Yang feels that most Chinese exercise for health rather than beauty, and, with the exception of the upper class, that attitude will stay. "But now I think people are experiencing the side effects of being rich, such as eating too much," he says, referring to Beijing's growing problem with obesity. But Yang feels it's all part of development. "Maybe some people have to die before other people realize there's a problem."

The business of tourism

China is now the world's third most popular tourist destination, and is expected to reach number one in 2020. But travelers still encounter a lot of *mafan* (trouble). Arranging tickets, hotels and reservations can be prohibitively difficult, and tourist scams are on the rise. Beijing has a love-hate relationship with tourism. The Chinese that work at tourist sites can seem pushy, aggressive, and rude, but Westerners buying fruit from a local market or mule cart can be embarrassed at how little they pay.

▲ Rickshaw drivers wait for tourist trade in the *hutong* areas surrounding Houhai Lake. Tourism is providing many new employment opportunities.

Preserving the culture

The tourist industry supports some illicit activities, such as the illegal taxis and unlicensed tour guides found near palaces and temples, but there are positives, too. In 2000, the city government was planning to demolish most of the old city's *siheyuan/ hutong* housing (see page 26). However, these areas were exactly what foreigners wanted to see. Areas that had been earmarked for destruction became tourist attractions, with *hutong* tours, restaurants, hotels, and even coffee shops with wireless Internet.

The emphasis on tourism gave *siheyuan* owners a new source of income. However, some Beijingers feel that turning a *siheyuan* into a coffee shop with wireless Internet access isn't preserving Chinese culture. Opinions differ as to which is better, preserving traditional housing to appeal to Western tourists, or tearing it down altogether and building high-rises to house Beijing's expanding population. Tourism is saving the buildings, but no one knows if it's really saving the culture.

▼ Visitors to the Forbidden City are dressed in traditional court costume to have their photograph taken.

Shi TaoTao and tea culture

Like many middle class Chinese, Shi TaoTao was a reluctant accounting student, as accounting has long been considered a fast track to a good job. She took up film editing for fun and became a documentary filmmaker for China Education Television (CETV). "All my interviews were in teahouses," she explains. "I like the tea culture, but not the teahouses. I knew my teahouse would be better." Bored with television, TaoTao studied tea culture and rented a space across from the Confucian Temple on Beijing's oldest street. "I wanted to create a center for Chinese culture." Her tea ceremony uses the same movements as everyone else's, but

she incorporates Tang Dynasty poetry and Confucian sayings—in Chinese, English, and Japanese. Her teahouse plays traditional Chinese music, not Western muzak on Chinese instruments. In the afternoons it's filled with Western temple visitors; in the evenings, it's host to Chinese artists, actors, poets, Confucian scholars, and Buddhist monks. "Tea culture is over 5,000 years old," she says. "If you study tea history, you know Chinese history."

◀ An employee prepares tea samples for customers to taste at a shop in "Tea Street," an area in Beijing dedicated to the retail and wholesale of teas from all over China.

The Beijing environment

Beijing suffers from both natural and manmade environmental problems. Its arid climate makes it vulnerable to sandstorms and perpetual water shortage, while its rapid development is creating pollution and straining what few resources it has. Fortunately, experts are starting to take action—and because of the 2008 Olympics the Beijing government is listening.

Sandstorms

Wars, land misuse, overpopulation, and rapid urbanization have all caused the haphazard clearing of trees in the area around Beijing, leading to desertification and soil erosion, which costs China US$6.5 billion–9.1 billion every year in lost agricultural revenue. Sand dunes 43 miles to the north are slowly drifting south toward the city, and serious storms have blown sand from north China to Korea, Japan, and even as far as California.

In response to the problem, farming has been regulated, and the government has reforested 110,000 acres of land in northern China. The 165,000 acres of trees planted between Beijing and the neighboring city of Tianjin should absorb 16.5 million tons of sand annually.

Pollution

A bigger problem than sand and dust storms is the production of the pollutants sulfur dioxide and nitrous oxide, from factories, coal stoves, and cars. Major industrial pollution is decreasing but car emissions are getting worse, due both to increased private car ownership and to rising global oil prices—China now buys cheaper and more polluting "sour oil" with a higher level of sulfur.

Local experts insist the city's air is better and skies are bluer, citing a 32.5 percent decrease in pollutants in 2004 from 1998. But, by the middle of the day, a dirty dishwater-colored haze obscures the view of buildings and the mountains. Beijing is now widely regarded as one of the most polluted cities in the world.

▲ Street sweepers struggle to keep pace with the amount of dust in the Beijing environment generated by sandstorms and the present construction boom.

▲ Smoggy morning traffic on one of the busy roads encircling Beijing. Air pollution is a worsening problem.

Wang Xiamen and green rooftops

As an aeronautical engineer, then a philosophy professor, Wang Xiamen never felt that he achieved anything. Now, as Secretary-General of China Environment Protection Foundation (CEPF), he is landscaping Beijing's roofs. "Roof gardens absorb dust particles, purify the air, protect roofs, conserve energy, and improve drainage," he explains. Plants absorb glare and city noise, and serve as natural insulation—saving cities tens of millions in energy costs. Roof gardens also combat the "urban heat island" effect. "Large scale landscaping can lower city temperatures by 10 degrees in the summer," says Wang. And at US$1.72 per square foot, it's cheaper than relocating factories.

Green rooftop projects also provide neighborhoods with much needed business, employment, and volunteer opportunities—and Wang feels he's finally making a contribution. "When I retired, I thought staying home would make me crazy," he said. Now 65, he visits work sites and climbs buildings. "I'm doing a good thing, and I'm making a little money," he says. "I'm happy."

▲ Wang Xiamen standing in a completed garden on top of a government building created by the China Environmental Protection Foundation's Green Rooftop Landscape Project.

The climate

Beijing has hot summers and cold, dry winters. The average temperature in January is 23°F (–5°C), but it has been recorded as low as 9°F (–23°C). The highest recorded summer temperature is 109°F (43°C). Coupled with high humidity and poor air quality, this can make life in the city very uncomfortable.

▶ Average temperatures and rainfall for Beijing.

Rainfall (mm)

Temperature

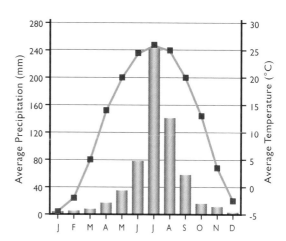

Dry Beijing

In 1949 the Miyun Reservoir was built to supply enough drinking water to the cities of Beijing and Tianjin and also Hebei province. In 1954 the nearby Guanting Reservoir was completed. Together they could provide 792 billion gallons of water per year, and an additional 15 reservoirs constructed in the following years should have ensured that no one went thirsty.

▶ The Yongding River dried up when a reservoir was built nearby and redirected the water. Beijing has relied on redirecting water to meet its needs, but the long term environmental effects could be disastrous.

No more water

Today, most of those reservoirs are polluted or have dried up. Miyun and Guanting together yield only 132 billion gallons. Water use has increased dramatically in Beijing, with domestic use alone almost doubling from 17 gallons per person per day in 1988 to nearly 32 gallons by 2001. This forces Beijing to divert water from the arid Hebei and Shanxi provinces—which have none to spare. Industry continues to use groundwater, which causes subsidence (sinking) as the land dries out, damaging city buildings, and experts think many water tables will be drained down to bedrock by 2016.

Beijing's population has grown by 11 million since 1949. Continued development of the city means further construction and an increase in heavy industry, both of which consume and pollute water. As the incomes of the people of Beijing have risen, so has their demand for water. Furthermore, leaky pipes waste over 20 percent of all transferred water.

◀ Pressure on water supplies means that extravagant uses such as washing cars could soon become more costly as prices go up.

The solution

Beijing is now imposing fines on polluters, distributing free taps that reduce water use, recycling more water, and discussing raising water prices to discourage overuse. A massive North-South Transfer Project will bring water from the water-rich Hubei province in the south, 600 miles away, to the parched northeast. In spite of its cost (US$58 billion) and the relocation of 400,000 people along its route, experts see this as the only viable long term solution. The project will see three major canals, each over 800 miles long, linking the major rivers of China with the dry lands of the north. The main central canal should be providing water to Beijing after 2010, but the whole project is not due for completion until the middle of the century, by which time the canals should supply the

▲ The construction of new canals similar to this one on the outskirts of Beijing will help to alleviate the city's water shortages.

north of China with 11.8 trillion gallons of water a year.

Not all action to ensure water supplies needs to be on a giant scale. Action by local citizens can also help. In 2001 a soy sauce factory was polluting the historically important Houhai Lake. A group of 23 residents took pictures, interviewed locals, confronted factory management, and began a letter-writing campaign to local government, which eventually relocated the polluting factory. Remarkably, these concerned citizens were 11 years old.

CASE STUDY

World Wildlife Foundation's Education Initiative for Water

World Wildlife Foundation's (WWF) Education Initiative for Water (EIW) is the future of environmental education and the brainchild of Zhang Yi, WWF's Education Program Officer. But water is just the beginning. "It's about introducing a new way of teaching and learning," she says. "The teachers use the water and community as a context for teaching. Traditionally in China, teachers talk and students listen. We're trying to teach another way."

Nature-loving Zhang Yi received a Master of Science degree in Environmental and Developmental Education before coming to WWF. "For the past eight years I've been trying to promote education for sustainable development, and put it in the schools," she says. EIW has been a success

with students, parents, and especially teachers. "They love being on an equal level with students," says Zhang. "There's a lot they can explore together." But even more important is citizen development. "We're teaching people how to take action to improve the environment."

Wastewater and recycling

Until the North-South Transfer Project is fully completed (see page 53), Beijing, which runs out of useable water every 10 months, will need to continue to divert water from neighboring provinces. In an attempt to slow the rate of this water diversion, several different steps are being taken. Polluted lakes, rivers, and reservoirs are being cleaned. The recycling of wastewater is also starting. Beijing could extract 18 billion to 39 billion gallons from rainfall and 170 billion gallons from recycled wastewater each year.

Wastewater treatment

The Jingcheng Recycled Water Company produces 131 million gallons of water daily, but wastewater treatment plants use three to four gallons of raw water to create one gallon of purified water. Having inefficient wastewater treatment plants means large amounts of wastewater are discharged without being treated, polluting rivers and groundwater. Beijing's water usage is only 10 percent recycled water, compared with 50 percent in developed countries. Untreated wastewater pollutes soil and groundwater; repairing the damage costs 20 times more than preventing the problem.

But wastewater technology is a rapidly growing field, attracting a wide range of both experts and investment. Beijing is constructing new plants, improving existing technology, and fixing leaky pipelines. By 2008, China's capital will be treating 90 percent of its urban sewage, and using 50 percent recycled water.

▼ A couple sorts through waste and separates it into different materials so they can transport it to a recycling center and sell it for reuse.

▲ A cleaner skims Houhai Lake for surface pollution as part of a cleanup of the city's waste. Water quality has been declining as the city has grown.

Household waste

The 15 million people in Beijing create mountains of household waste—1.2 million tons annually in the central urban areas alone. Besides taking up space, untreated trash in landfills causes serious soil and groundwater pollution. Recycling programs today consist largely of elderly people sifting through garbage cans, or migrant workers circling neighborhoods, calling for refuse. But Beijing has begun waste-sorting programs and is building 1,800 recycling stations, planning for a 30 percent recycle rate by 2008.

▶ A recycling station where waste is separated into its various materials for reprocessing and sale.

CASE STUDY

Dr. Zhang Huichun, wastewater treatment

"If you want a sustainable economy, you can't pollute the environment," says Dr. Zhang Huichun, owner of Greentech Engineering. Zhang, who has degrees in hydrogeology, hydraulics, and environmental studies, uses biomass to treat wastewater and destroy pollutants. What is biomass?

"You grow a special kind of bacteria, depending on the type of waste," says Zhang. "The bacteria eat the pollutants and eventually sink to the bottom." Treated water is drained off the surface; the remaining bacteria, or sludge, is dried, compressed into cakes, and sold as fertilizer, fuel, or even building material.

Technology is racing ahead—one reason the environmental field is known as a "morning business" in China and holds special appeal for Zhang. "Business is challenging," he says. "But to be involved with something growing so fast, and that's also good for the environment, that's ideal. After all, if you have a lot of money, but no drinking water, your standard of living will suffer."

The Beijing of tomorrow

For the Chinese government, Beijing, as China's international showcase, must be seen to be prosperous, open, and developed. As China's seat of national power, it should remain stable, controlled, and above all, Chinese. Blending these elements is difficult enough, but add in a large and dense population, haphazard development, very bad pollution, and a shortage of natural resources, and Beijing's future might look bleak. Much like the Chinese *yin* and *yang* idea of balance, Beijing must balance its many opposing forces to prosper in a globalized world.

2008 Olympics

The Chinese are proud of their long, glorious history, and ashamed of their current underdeveloped status. Rapid economic growth is not enough; the country feels compelled to prove that it is a global player, worthy of the world's respect. That opportunity is coming, with the 2008 Olympics.

Beijing's desire to show it is "as good as the West" has sent development into overdrive. But by-products such as pollution and water shortages could mean future economic hardship, and as more national resources are diverted to Beijing, more unemployed workers will follow. Forced relocation and a skyrocketing cost of living mean that many Beijingers are pushed to society's outer edges, even as the economy continues to grow.

Sustainable development

Beijing's current pattern of consumption is not sustainable. The city can't build roads fast enough to add 2,000 new cars a week. Beijing can't keep taking water from local agricultural areas to supply a city that allows health spas and golf courses unlimited water supplies. In an important and significant change the Beijing

▼ The countdown to the Beijing Olympics of 2008 has proven a major stimulus to a wide range of developments in the city.

▲ A mother and daughter walk across Tiananmen Square on November 5, 2005, the smoggiest day ever recorded in Beijing at the time. Such days are a clear warning that Beijing cannot continue to develop unchecked.

authorities are listening to their people—holding public hearings and consulting with experts, engaging in free debate and experimentation, and supporting grassroots environmental movements. Beijing's desire for international credibility has caused some decisions to be taken without proper consideration, but has also led to closer observation of Western problems—and their solutions.

Beijing megalopolis

Some of Beijing's short-term goals include doubling the city's annual economic output, increasing the private and service sectors' share in economic activities, and increasing people's disposable income. Long-term plans are more ambitious, however. One of Tiananmen Square's most popular attractions is the giant Olympic clock, counting down to 2008. But some look to the Beijing megalopolis of 2020, the future home to 18 million people. The plan is to transform today's satellite towns into 11 urbanized cities, with universities, high-quality hospitals, theaters, and sports stadiums, as well as high-tech industries and factories, and rail lines for those who still need to commute. The key is to keep all areas diverse, with people of different jobs and incomes living together, so one area isn't vacated even as another prospers. The megalopolis won't change the face of central Beijing, but it will ease the burden on resources and ensure further sustainable development for the city, in the 21st century and beyond.

▲ Huairou, a 90-minute drive northeast of central Beijing, is one of the new satellite areas that form Beijing's vision of the future.

Glossary

Autonomous Regions Regions in China that are similar to provinces, but have a higher concentration of minority peoples.

Chinese New Year China's most important holiday. Because travel is so expensive, this is often the only time families can get together.

communism A political theory that advocates a society where all property is shared, and people work and are paid according to their ability and need.

Communist Party of China (CPC) China's ruling political party, which has been in power since 1949, when the People's Republic of China (PRC) was founded under Mao Zedong.

Cultural Revolution A period (1966–76) when the Chinese government tried to make everyone in society equal. Manual laborers rather than educated professionals were honored, and land and goods were taken from their owners and redistributed.

Confucian Relating to the Chinese philosopher Confucius (551–479B.C.E.), who had a strong influence on Asian culture.

desertification The degradation of previously fertile land into desert because of drought, deforestation, or poor farming methods.

intellectual property A work or invention that is the result of creativity, such as a film or manuscript, which may be protected by patent or copyright law.

mainlanders Chinese who live on mainland China, not in Hong Kong, Macao, or Taiwan.

megalopolis A very large, continuous urban area made up of a collection of adjacent towns and cities.

multinational corporation A business that has direct investment and trade in two or more countries.

nitrous oxide A gas associated with smog that is found in automotive exhaust.

nongovernmental organization (NGO) An organization that performs work for the public, such as fighting poverty, but does not belong to any government.

reparations Payments or other contributions to make amends for a wrong one has done, usually made by the losing side of a war.

research and development (R&D) In industry, work directed toward the innovation, introduction, and improvement of products and processes.

satellite city A smaller city closely connected to a larger, neighboring city, designed to encourage people to move out of the city center, and ease congestion.

special economic zone A region whose economic laws are different from those of the rest of the country (usually through tax breaks for foreign investment).

sulfur dioxide Another pollutant gas found in car exhaust.

tai chi A Chinese system of slow meditative physical exercise designed for relaxation, achieving balance and health.

tea ceremony The traditional movements, sayings, and culture associated with drinking certain types of tea; called *cha dao* in Chinese.

warlord Usually a regional military commander with his own army and individual autonomy.

World Trade Organization (WTO) An international body founded in 1995 to promote economic development by reducing tariffs and other restrictions on trade.

yin **and** *yang* The traditional Chinese concept of opposite qualities in balance, symbolized by a black and white circle.

Further information

Web sites

The Beijing Guide
http://www.thebeijingguide.com/
A site offering panoramic shots of Beijing attractions, along with Chinese phrases, music, and humor to illustrate local culture.

Beijing International
http://www.ebeijing.gov.cn/default.htm
The city's official Web site, which includes tips on day-to-day living in Beijing, such as how to bargain, how to lease a house, and rules for keeping a pet.

Lonely Planet World Guide: Beijing
http://www.lonelyplanet.com/worldguide/
destinations/asia/china/beijing/
Quick travel and cultural information.

Books

Baldwin, Robert F. *Daily Life in Ancient and Modern Beijing.* Minneapolis: Runestone Press, 1999. A brief, illustrated study of social life and customs in the city, for readers grades 4 to 7.

Du Feibao and Du Bai. *Things Chinese.* Beijing: China Travel and Tourism Press, 2002. A popular book explaining the folklore behind everyday Chinese customs.

Fodor's Beijing and Shanghai. New York: Fodor's Travel Publications, 2005. An informative guide to Beijing's attractions.

Ma Yan. *The Diary of Ma Yan.* New York: HarperCollins, 2005. The diary of a real Chinese girl who is determined to get an education despite hardships.

Xu Chengbei. *Old Beijing: In the Shadow of the Imperial Throne.* Beijing: Foreign Language Press, 2001. An illustrated history of the city from 3,000 years ago through 1949.

Xu Chengbei. *Old Beijing: People, Houses and Lifestyles.* Beijing: Foreign Language Press, 2001. Descriptions of the day-to-day lives of ordinary people in Beijing's past, generously illustrated.

Index